NEW TECHNOLOGY
IN THE
CIVIL WAR

ISBN-13: 978-0-15-352937-5
ISBN-10: 0-15-352937-7

10   1083   14 13
4500436070

Harcourt
SCHOOL PUBLISHERS

Visit *The Learning Site!* www.harcourtschool.com

THE WAR OF FIRSTS

"What's that?"

People asked this question in 1861, when they spotted a hot-air balloon floating near the White House. A man named Thaddeus Lowe was showing President Abraham Lincoln how balloons could be used in the war that had just started.

Balloons were not the only example of technology used in a new way during the Civil War. Railroads helped move troops quickly. Telegraphs helped officers stay in touch. Doctors and nurses learned much more about germs and the importance of cleanliness. Ambulances moved wounded soldiers for the first time.

Many weapons were also used for the first time, such as ironclad ships, machine guns, and rifles that could shoot great distances. These weapons changed the way wars were fought, making this war between free states and slave states the bloodiest in United States history.

Steam-powered ironclads were first used in the Civil War.

THE PRESIDENTIAL INVENTOR

Abraham Lincoln was especially interested in new technology because he himself was an inventor. In 1849, he received a patent for an invention used to help raise riverboats over sandbars. He built his own model and is the only United States President to have a patent.

Patent No. 6469 was granted in 1849 to Abraham Lincoln.

The Civil War was also the first war to be photographed. Americans were shocked by photographs taken after battles. They could see how terrible the war was. At the same time, families were grateful to find photographs of their loved ones in letters mailed from the battlefield.

All this technology was exciting and would improve people's lives after the war. It forever changed the ways that people traveled, communicated, and stayed healthy.

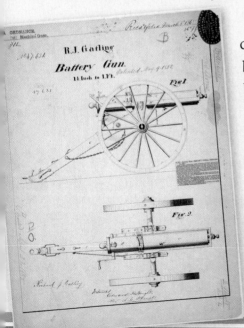

The Civil War was both an old and a new kind of war. It was an old war because soldiers used older weapons, but both sides also used new technology. Civil War expert Shelby Foote said, "The Civil War defined us as what we are, and it opened us to being what we became, good and bad things."

The Civil War saw new kinds of weapons.

3

TRANSPORTATION AND COMMUNICATION

Union troops in Georgia needed more soldiers in 1863. In 11 days, 20,000 Union soldiers were rushed 1,200 miles from Virginia to a site near Chattanooga, Tennessee. Instead of traveling by foot or on horseback, they rode in trains.

The North had more than twice as many miles of train tracks as the South. When railroad companies there argued about the cost of transporting soldiers and supplies, Congress passed a law giving the President more powers over railroads.

In the South, on the other hand, many different companies owned the railroads. Often the tracks were of different widths. This made moving troops and supplies over long distances difficult.

The Civil War was the first war in which trains were widely used to transport soldiers and supplies.

President Lincoln visited the War Department's Telegraph Office every day to get the latest news.

Like railroad tracks, telegraph wires and cables had also begun to crisscross the country. Samuel Morse had invented the telegraph by 1844. For the first time, news could travel faster than people.

More than 15,000 miles of new telegraph lines were laid for the military during the Civil War. Government and military leaders could give orders and get information more quickly than ever before.

In 1861, the U.S. Military Telegraph Service was formed. During the war, there were more than 2,000 telegraph operators in the United States. More than half ended up working for this service.

COMMUNICATION PROBLEMS

The telegraph improved communication during the war, but there were problems. Sometimes operators gave orders to troops before waiting for orders from military officers. Another problem was wiretapping. Both the North and the South spied on each other's telegraph systems.

A telegraph station

MIGHTIER WEAPONS OF WAR

Many new weapons were used in the Civil War. One of the most important was the long-range rifle, which could send bullets as far as 1,500 feet. (Older-style muskets could shoot about 300 feet.) Both the Union and the Confederacy used these rifles. They accounted for more than 90 percent of the war's wounds and deaths. Bayonets, long a part of warfare, were no match against the accuracy and long range of the new rifles.

A new type of bullet made long-range weapons even deadlier. This bullet was called the "minié ball" after its inventor, Claude Minié of France. Weighing about

New weapons meant that more soldiers were hurt or killed in the Civil War than in previous wars.

1 ounce, the minié spun at great speed out of the weapon and could be loaded far faster than previous rifle bullets. Some historians say this bullet was one of the most important technological developments in nineteenth-century warfare.

The Union army used several types of repeating rifles, or rifles that could be loaded with more than one bullet at a time. Some of these could fire as many as 14 shots within a minute. One Union soldier said, "They say we are not fair, that we have guns that we load up on Sunday and shoot all the rest of the week."

The Gatling gun

The Confederates had their own breakthrough: the first machine-gun–type weapon ever used in a war. The Williams breech-loading rapid-fire gun could fire at a rate of 65 rounds per minute. The Gatling gun, later used by the Union, was capable of firing 600 rounds per minute.

Confederates used mines and torpedoes to try to sink Union ships. Many small cast-iron torpedoes were painted to look like pieces of coal. Confederate torpedoes sank 7 Union ironclads, 22 wooden gunboats, and 14 other Union ships.

The biggest explosion of the Civil War was caused by a Confederate torpedo disguised as a box of candles.

Wounded soldiers receiving medical care on the battlefield

DOCTOR, DOCTOR!

Sometimes the care that injured soldiers received during the war made them worse, or even killed them. Military hospitals during the Civil War were often dirty. Germs spread quickly. Antibiotics had not yet been discovered.

Despite these problems, medical advances were made or improved upon during the Civil War. Anesthesia had been developed in the 1840s. By the time of the Civil War, it was used in 95 percent of operations.

At the time, surgeons often washed their hands and operating tools *after* an operation, not before. Infection was widespread. In 1861, the United States Sanitary Commission was created to help make Union camps and hospitals cleaner.

Jonathan Letterman, medical director of the Union's Army of the Potomac, became known as the "Father of American Battlefield Medicine." At the start of the war, wounded soldiers were sometimes left on the battlefield for days. Letterman created this country's first ambulance corps, using horse-and-wagon teams. At the Battle of Antietam, Letterman's ambulances removed the North's wounded from the battlefield within 24 hours.

Letterman also developed a system for treating soldiers that included a battlefront medical station, a small hospital area close by for emergencies, and a larger hospital away from the fighting. Letterman's three-level system is still used today.

The Civil War also prompted drug research and the creation of drug companies. The Union blocked supplies from reaching the South, so the Confederates hired scientists and doctors to find substitute medicines.

Before Jonathan Letterman developed ambulances, there was no system for getting injured soldiers off battlefields.

SHOWDOWN ON THE WATER

Before the Civil War, ships were made mostly of wood and were powered by the wind. In the mid-1800s, navies in Europe and the United States began to build stronger boats of iron, called ironclads. Ironclads were driven by steam engines and screw propellers.

When the Civil War started, the Confederacy had no navy. It quickly started building and buying ships. Its masterpiece, the *Virginia*, was built from the wreck of an abandoned Union ship called the USS *Merrimack*. Confederate engineers turned it into an ironclad, stronger than anything the Union had. One person described it as a "floating barn roof."

The Union hired an inventor named John Ericsson to stop the *Virginia*. He came up with the *Monitor*, a new iron-clad design. It was part boat and part submarine.

The *Monitor* vs. the *Virginia*		
About the *Monitor*		About the *Virginia*
776 tons	**Weight**	3,200 tons
172 feet	**Length**	275 feet
41 feet, 6 inches	**Beam**	38 feet, 6 inches
11 feet, 4 inches	**Hull Height**	27 feet, 6 inches
8 knots	**Speed**	9 knots
59 crew members	**Crew**	320 crew members

The meeting of the two ironclads is sometimes called the battle between the *Monitor* and the *Merrimack*.

SUBMARINES

Both sides built submarines during the Civil War. The Union built the USS *Alligator,* which was lost during an 1863 storm before seeing combat. The Confederacy's sub, the *H.L. Hunley,* launched a torpedo and sank a Union ship off the South Carolina coast in 1864. However, the *Hunley* and its crew sank at the same time. The submarine and its crew's remains were recovered in 2000.

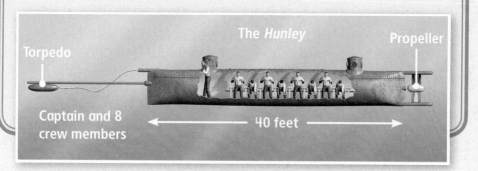

The *Hunley*

Torpedo

Propeller

Captain and 8 crew members

40 feet

On March 9, 1862, crowds gathered on the shore of the James River at Hampton Roads, Virginia, to watch the first battle between two ironclads. The day before, the *Virginia* had defeated several wooden Union ships, showing that the old boats were no match for ironclads. In the course of about four hours, the *Virginia* and the *Monitor* ran into each other five times. The battle ended with no real winner, however.

The battle was a turning point in naval history, marking the change from an old era to a new. It remains one of the most famous naval battles in history.

Neither ship lasted long. Two months later, Confederates blew up the *Virginia* at Norfolk, Virginia, rather than surrender the boat to the enemy. The *Monitor* sank in a storm off the coast of North Carolina on December 31, 1862.

UP IN THE AIR: BALLOONS

When Thaddeus Lowe launched his hot-air balloon in Washington in 1861, he sent a telegraph message to President Lincoln saying: "I have pleasure in sending you this first dispatch ever telegraphed from an aerial station."

Lincoln was so impressed that he created the Union's Balloon Corps. In September 1861, Lowe rose 1,000 feet in a balloon over Virginia, across the Potomac River from Washington, D.C. He telegraphed reports that Confederate troops were 3 miles away. The Union opened fire. As a result, for the first time in history, troops were able to shoot at enemy troops without being able to see them. At Yorktown, Virginia, in 1862, and later at Fredericksburg, Lowe sent reports from the air about Confederate troops.

The Confederates began to try to trick Union balloon-ists by setting up fake camps and by keeping real camps dark at night.

The envelope holds the air.

Burners send heat up inside the envelope.

A BALLOONING SPY?

Thaddeus Lowe hoped to try to cross the Atlantic Ocean in a balloon. In 1861, he flew from Ohio to South Carolina, traveling 900 miles in nine hours. His timing was unlucky. A week earlier, the Civil War had begun. The Confederates were sure he was a Yankee spy. Lowe explained that he was innocent. In just a few months, however, Lowe became the Union's "chief aeronaut."

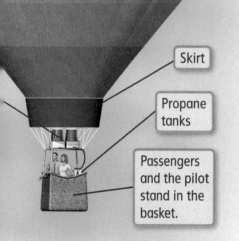

Hot air is released through the parachute valve to make the balloon rise or descend.

Skirt

Propane tanks

Passengers and the pilot stand in the basket.

Hot-air balloons can fly because hot air is lighter than cooler air and rises.

The Confederacy also ordered a few balloons of its own. In Yorktown, Virginia, a Confederate captain rose into the air and drew a quick map of Union troops. Then the balloon broke loose. Confederates thought he was the enemy and started shooting, but the captain was not hurt.

The Confederacy ordered two more balloons. The only available gas was in Richmond, so one balloon was filled there and pulled by train and tugboat to battle; the other stayed near Richmond.

By 1863, a general with whom Lowe worked was ordered to leave. His replacement did not care about balloons and cut funding for them. Lowe quit, and the Balloon Corps ended.

SEEING THE WAR: PHOTOGRAPHY

In 1862, photographer Mathew Brady had a photography show in New York called "The Dead of Antietam." There were pictures of dead soldiers at the Civil War's worst battle. People were shocked. They could not believe their eyes.

People had never seen war photographs. Photography in the United States was only about 20 years old when the war started. The Civil War was the first war documented by photos. Americans began to see what war was really like.

During the Civil War, photographers took several hundred thousand pictures. Photographers made money by taking pictures for soldiers to send home. Photographers could not take battle or "action" shots, however. Camera lenses had to be open for 10 to 30 seconds, and subjects had to stand still during that time.

Mathew Brady opened his studio in Washington, D.C., in 1856.

Soldiers posed for photographs printed on small cards. Soldiers often included the photos in their letters.

14

Photography allowed people to see what was going on during the Civil War.

Instead of taking battle shots, photographers took pictures of things that were not moving, such as soldiers and leaders posing for portraits, buildings and parked ambulances, and battlefields after a battle. Some soldiers were photographed for medical purposes, to show injuries or completed operations.

Many photographers shot Civil War pictures, but Mathew Brady is the most famous. Brady took many pictures himself, but he also hired photographers to follow troops. He managed the photographers, collected their pictures, and preserved their work. Many photos with his name on them were taken by other photographers.

After the war, people became less interested in Civil War photographs. Brady died broke in 1875. He would be pleased to know that historians today value his work highly.

Think and Respond

1. How did telegraphs change wars?

2. Why was anesthesia important during the Civil War?

3. How were hot-air balloons useful in the Civil War?

4. Why were there few, if any, photographs taken of battle scenes during the Civil War?

5. Why was the battle between the *Monitor* and the *Virginia* so significant?

 # Activity

Advances in technology have many consequences. Think about the changes brought about by new technologies developed during the Civil War. In your opinion, which changes were positive? Which technologies had negative consequences? Make a chart of positive and negative consequences of technology. Be prepared to defend your opinions.